EVEN THE AUTUMN LEAVES
Story Poems

Harry Youtt

For Everyone who is part of MY story poem

TABLE OF CONTENTS

EVEN THE AUTUMN LEAVES
(Story Poems)

Harry Youtt

INTRODUCTION

This collection is mostly story poems. Several of the poems have appeared before in previous collections of mine. Several have had their initial outings in various literary journals, but most will be new to you.

Story Poems. Each poem carries a narrative that takes readers from point A to point B and so on through the telling of something that seems to have happened in the world. This alone would make it a radical collection in the eyes of modern poetry. Most Modernist poets, because they somehow seem to have taken a sworn oath and genuflected toward obscurity, manage to evade narratives that make sense and lead to something. If you're looking for poems that tell stories, then you've come to the right place. If instead you're looking to be stupefied by blind alleys that keep you confused about whether the poet had a message to communicate or a direction to take you, then this is not a collection for you.

Someone once criticized a poem I presented at a reading by telling me I didn't understand modern poetry. According to him (and I think he's right) the purpose of Modernist poetry is usually to hide the ball artfully from the reader. This leaves readers free to make what they want of any poetic phrasing and gives them ambiguities to discuss with their friends. This also provides essential material for the so-called *close readings* that become the grist for poetry comprehension workshops. I replied I wasn't into hiding the ball in my poem. My purpose was simply to reveal that figurative *ball* with all its blemishes and shadings and follow it in its meanderings as it rolled through the poem to where I thought it wanted to take me. And along the way perhaps, I hoped to polish the ball to make it glisten and glimmer a little, so people would notice its nuances.

This confession of course deprives me of any hope

the Modernists or the Post-Modernists will ever welcome me into their camps. All well and good. I'm hoping you'll stay for the narratives, even though the poem-stories are just going to come straight at you.

The collection gets its title from my poem of the same name: *Even the Autumn Leaves*, which is one of the poems in my *Elderverses* collection. I like that phrase because of its manifold possible meanings, all of which are explored in the body of the poem:

> *Even the autumn leaves remember the springtime*
> *everyone else is not quite forgetting,*
> *folding into cedar chests, crossing from lists.*

I'm hoping that variety of possibilities that stem from the title will continue to remind everone that our language, in an out of poetry, carries dazzling possibilities of meaning.

I've included a short section that contains a separate poem about each of my four grandchildren. My grandchildren, like all grandchildren, are separte stories in themselves. These are story-poems from early in their careers as humans.

The collection concludes with a very short section I call *Two Sweat-Vision Poems*. They give me an opportunity to speculate and explore a couple of visions that go a step beyond the limits of story narrative.

Because the poems in the collection are, each of them, separate stories, I'm suggesting it might be a good idea to limit yourelves to reading not more than a few of them at a single sitting, even though most of them aren't long. They just go off in different directions.

EVEN THE AUTUMN LEAVES

Even the autumn leaves
turn colors more vivid
than what was imagined in summer.

Even the autumn leaves remain for a time,
brilliant new visions
blazing into the year's final season.

Even the autumn leaves, now nearly brown,
crackle underfoot brittle, withering,
soon to be swept into forever.

Even the autumn leaves remember the springtime
everyone else is not quite forgetting,
folding into cedar chests, crossing from lists.

Even the autumn leaves enjoy waning warmth
of sunshine-days that shorten
into winter we never saw coming.

Even the autumn leaves, on brink of disappearance,
bitter implication of harvest afterthought:
grapes, corn, pumpkins, *even* the autumn leaves.

Even the autumn — leaves, syntax changing
before our eyes, noun becoming exit-verb
as if by magic, season disappearing into winter.

Now *Even* — by itself, flutters finally alone,
crumbles into multiple meanings,
expands into actual *evening*, end of a day.

Even - by itself some sort of leveling word
a cutting-off, all of us down at last to common size,
as a reaper would cut: *even*, right here at the ending.

Story Poems

TWENTY-ONE BALLOONS

Twenty-One Balloons, late afternoon, descending,
each one striped and banded and color-patched
the way a kid would do it at a long-ago easel,
tongue wagging, smock smeared with poster paint.

Lulling me valley-ward, open-mouthed and
making my way down-highway from the Chiriaco pass,
(that desolate high-dust plain where the gruff Patton
trained *real men* in another age
to weather the dust, and buffet about in tanks).

Twenty-One balloons descend in silent invasion,
me, barreling down that long-glide
toboggan-ride, skateboard-surprise of a
sweeping hill that tumbles you into the parch
of that California desert town, Indio,

sprawled in the broad cleavage between
those great peaks of San Jacinto and San Gorgonio,
where wind on some days but not today
sweeps hard and loud from the west,
just down from the vast field of windmills
that would drive a thousand Don Quixotes
even madder than everything that had come before.

Twenty-One balloons descending
into just-before-dinner-time Indio.
Coming down the way the day comes down,
one-by-one relentlessly setting
a step or two ahead of me – and the twilight,
in stillness that only moments ago became golden.

As if each one of the twenty-one balloons
is a piece on a dazzling game board,
being slid gently from its place at play,
and boxed carefully for tomorrow
by sleepy-eyed players reluctant to give in.

DATE SHAKES

Speaking of calories, there were date shakes
in the heart of Mojave, almost into Death Valley,
every day at the early end of sunlight,
date shakes, cold and thick
and slumping out of a tipped glass in your direction.

First you had to get there from dusty Shoshone,
over to Tecopa, still more dust everywhere,
and then you had to find your way to the turn-off
and the sign that says *China Ranch*,
which is tricky. But it's never tricky for Mala;

he always finds the road, he always knows,
even though you can't see the Ranch yet
as the road winds around rocks
and down, gradual, into a gully,
getting greener and greener on your way,

past cottonwoods and willows
and then groves of date palms
cultivated in rows.
Oasis beside the Amargosa River
not far from the canyon.

Ranch buildings, a green house, and even a shop
where you can buy any kind of dates they grow,
gathered in baskets,
and where you can order one of those
date shakes I told you about.

From a table full of gathered dates,
they chop some into a plastic bin
and scoop them into one of those
milk shake spinners with frozen custard

and spin it up cold and thick

into a glass they serve to you,
so it slumps down at your face
and into your mouth when you tilt the cup.
With sun slipping further down
between the rocks and the trees

and desert shadows
taking over
for fading December light.
Quiet China Ranch,
gullied there near the River

that makes this always a *valley of life*,
right there at *Death Valley's* edge,
and you know all this,
and you pray,
just before you take that first sip.

BASKETBALL PRIZES

"You again!" they'd say when they saw my father coming.
"You ought to come out when it's hot;
at least you might draw some customers!"

Once a year, every year, in August,
on a cold night when hardly anyone else was about,
my father would drive those ten dark miles
down the Lake Road, to that little Vermilion Town
and its dust-shabby Crystal Beach Amusement Park –
like a carnival that found a place it liked
and just stayed put.

There would be the smell of candy apples
and popcorn and cotton candy, and caramel,
and strung-barebulb-bright lights
and sometimes a faint smell of gunpowder
burnt at the shooting range.
Tired vendors in undershirts against the chill
standing at their stations, with little hope
that visitors would come to salvage a losing day.

And my father, with the carousel's
sad calliope background music,
would make his way straight to the game where,
for a quarter you got to shoot four basketballs up
at an undersized hoop, and the basketballs
would drop down onto a drooping net
and tumble back to where
you picked them up for another shot.
If you sank every shot you paid for,
you won your choice of the
high shelf table lamps and teddy bears.
Three out of four got you
second-shelf smaller stuffed animals

and porcelain planters.
Two got you a bottom-shelf souvenir item
and one out of four got you one of those
rush-woven finger traps
that when you slide your fingers in
and try to pull them out, you get stuck.

My father couldn't miss.
That's what made the basketball game guys crazy
They'd let him win a prize from every shelf,
only one. Then he'd have to leave.
And he couldn't come back until next year.

Every year. Once a year.
Teddy bears went to the neighborhood little kids.
An elbow-handled lamp with a parchment shade
stood on the kitchen table until
my mother moved to the Senior Apartments.

Me, I got a red wooden cane
with ceramic dog's head handle.
Probably from the bottom shelf.
I've carried it with me, and even now,
cane snapped off long ago,
the dog's head stands on a pedestal
I mounted on a wall.

And every time I squint my eyes at that dog's head,
I see my father's hands lining up
in his two handed set-shot stance,
his face concentrating and solemn,
in "the zone" long before anybody spoke of a "zone,"

and the basketball arc-ing into the night sky
disappearing in black space above the glare
of wired carnival light-bulb strings,

the ball finally reappearing to
swish through that hoop,
one perfect shot after another −
and that smell of caramel, popcorn and candy apples,
the sad face of the basketball game guy,
as my father, serious as always
collects his prizes and prepares to be banished
for another year, guilty of the crime of excellence
in a world that was never prepared for it.

A SOLITARY BROAD-BROWED CATFISH

High up the long-sweep
of rock and gristle mountain,
up from the sea past hazy crestlines,
one after another,

vapor-clouds thicken slowly
and mix themselves
into a swirling meringue soup
for the sun to set its yolk in.

And then, breeze-blown,
the cloud mass begins to wisp up
and spume into the dusky present,
like gowns of sultry Sirens bent upon mischief.

High up at the basined top
of that rock and gristle mountain,
is a single lily-padded pond —
black, and still.

And a solitary broad-browed catfish,
primordial white, and wily,
swims alone, only silence around him.
He knows to stay deep during daylight,

knows that only lesser fish are safe,
swishing tails together in sun-flicker ,
side-by-side-by-side,
believing in each other.

High up on that rock and gristle mountain,
the solitary broad-browed catfish
swims alone at dusk
and into the cover of breezy night,

looks up, once at the sky,
and the swirling cloud,
feels the rippling breeze
on his dorsal back,

eyes once the cloud,
and owns his solitary bliss.

LIGHTHOUSE

Lighthouse anchors the town of Lorain, always,
built way way out at the desolate breakwater's end,
as if it were the home of some eccentric family,
content to live a life apart
and guard against marauding monsters from the sea.

Solid, it looked to be carved out of rock,
rising three stories above its over-thick base,
the last place you'd ever think would disappear,
even in a perfect storm.

As a boy I dreamed of bringing my new family
back to live out there, my pretty wife and me,
with a brood of kids.
I'd teach my sons and my daughters
to fish for perch from the rails,
watching them feed flocking seagulls
with crumbs of old bread.

Lighthouse – mainstay of the city's definition.
Peaked red roof, even a brick chimney,
and of course, that Fresnel lantern cylinder,
set into that high railed walk atop the tower,
looking almost like the steeple on a chapel,
circling bright beam of beacon light
once every thirty seconds,
telling the world where to find us
from out of the dark.

Foghorn dormer, and big windows everywhere,
even up the tower, even an attic window,
just under the peak,
each framed by massive steel shutters
that really mean business when the going gets rough.

Davits and rails and gangways.

And at the sundown end of every humid summer day,
with nothing else moving,
and the lake flat as a silent mirror that tells no lies,
we'd all be sitting side by side on a wooden bench,
that family of mine as it grew.
Feet propped up on the rails,
watching the shore lights twinkle on,
so near and yet so far away,
wishing the whole town well,
and sweet dreams and easy rest,
as the rippling river surge,
lapped against the piers.

On whitecap days, freighters would hoot greetings
to everyone, and laundry would flap from clotheslines
rigged to the boat davit.
On nights of deep fog rolling,
the horns would harrumph their calls,
and my kids would sit quiet with my wife and me,
their night shirts bunched against the chill,
mouths agape and watching the thick of things together.

Out of the mist a ship would suddenly loom,
close enough to be reached out to and almost touched.
And a voice from the ship's bridge, booming:
"This would be the port of Lorain?"

"Yep, it is."
"Thank God."
Then hearing the sigh of the crew
at the sound of the news.

When storms came in,
I'd struggle from window to window,

figuring which steel shutters need closing for safety.
Then I'd go inside, pull the big steel door shut.
I'd build a fire in the fireplace.
Smoke would rise up the chimney.
We'd be singing songs and popping corn.
Marshmallows would be brought out,
at just the right moment.

And before I went to bed,
I'd haul up to the lantern tower
and double check the Fresnel beam,
just in case there were ships out there,
about to be lost at sea.
Then we'd all go to sleep
and never have to worry the scream of the wind
or the crash of the water.

When morning came the lake would be calming out,
like a wrinkled sheet that somebody was about to iron.
Bacon would be frying, with smell of toast browning,
and the town would still be there, always,
just the way I'd left it, before all the storms began.

PONDEROSAS

Twenty-seven proud Ponderosa Pines
strain to keep their green, in midst of
brown-needle, dry forest corpses.
Trees that own the country land I live on.

Now it's the dry-drought plague they struggle against,
watching distances where their brothers and sisters
burned in the fire last year
that almost took everything.

Now the bark beetles come,
tree by tree down the mountain, killing,
with everybody not quite knowing what it is
they should be doing to put a stop to things.

The pines at dusk, bending needles down,
like horses that nuzzle into buckets
we secretly carry out to them in the evening
– water, laced with plant food.

Branches creak, and we sense their concern
and the way they stand together against uncertainty,
saving strength, helpless to run deeper into the woods
like animals, hiding until danger is over.

For long moments we extend our arms
round their hard bark trunks
and feel their spirit sapping,
and the sway of life still inside.

When the wind rises we hear the pine trees
neigh and whinny together in unison.
The sound comes out like a comforting
whoosh, over the world,

assurance that things might come out right after all
– given enough patience and time
and blessing by God –
if indeed God listens to pine trees — or me –

comforting *whoosh* like the sea, like water
flowing over everything that is,
branching tails that swish away every pest –
prayer of the trees, prayer for rain,

One more green season into possibly forever.

I WAS NEVER A LAMB

The lamb, born Thursday
sleeps the sunny wind
all the way down,
chin and cheek snugged
onto his mother's back
as the green hill ruffles,
mother facing away
and thinking thoughts
of other pastures.

If I were a lamb,
that's where I'd be too.
I'd prop my chin on the broad curve
of her wooly-scruffy back
pretending at first to sleep,
but all the time sensing
how still she remained,
wishing me further slumber.

I'd imagine her tranquil eyes
as if they gazed at me
when I wasn't looking.
I'd know from the stillness
how subtle is a mother's love.

And I would sleep the whole afternoon
down into moonrise.
That is what I would do, if I were a lamb.

I was never a lamb.

POST-TRAUMATIC STRESS SURVIVOR
CELEBRATES THE 4TH OF JULY

"Don't be listening to me," he says.
"I can suck the sap out of any Independence Day.
And I don't even know
what any of that means anymore,
if I ever did.
You go on ahead and have some fun.
I might come down later."

Telling himself maybe there won't be another war;
maybe having done his part will serve to prevent it.
But he knows this isn't true,
and here is the flash and blam
beginning again that proves it.
There is the crowd again,
ooing and ahh-ing and hoping for more.

Him saying *who am I now?*
What is there left of me worth saving?
What is it that got me home?
Irony of an injured ear not bringing deafness
but only making loudness more intense.
Ears gone bad from the battles.
Can't even hear friends laugh in crowded rooms.

Mildewed uniform long ago discarded.
Cringing in a bedroom with each magnesium retort,
he sent his loved ones on to the parade without him,
only he doesn't ever go outside,
and maybe a daughter or a wife
will make her way back to the house

to brew a cup of coffee for him

or pop open the tab of a can of beer
and sit across a kitchen table trying to smile
or crouch to wrap an arm around a shoulder
as he shudders.

Stop the bombing altogether?
Just hold the fireworks, at least for this year?
Never gonna happen.
Not even an option.

THE PEELER GUY IN UNION SQUARE

The Peeler Guy in Union Square.
In his time — a legend.
Always in a fancy suit, a crisp shirt,
and almost always even a vest,
low to the pavement to demonstrate
how you could notch and peel a carrot,
and shape it like stars when you sliced it.

Crowds would form around him,
just to find out what the commotion was,
until they saw it was this elegant guy
hunkered on a camp stool,
with vegetable peelings all around him,
and they'd stay to listen and watch,
even if they didn't care that much for carrots.

Kind of a swarthy-dapper,
the look of a homeless guy,
but decked in those perfect clothes,
causing you to think, maybe his sister died
and left him some big money,
but he still kept coming to the park every day,
because that's where the good people were.

He probably didn't even have a sister.
He just knew how to pick his suits and shirts,
and he paid for them with what he earned
selling potato peelers, one by one
or better yet, five by five.

This is what he was —
before he wasn't anymore.

And the kids still come to look for him.
They'd bought one of those peelers
for Christmas one time, for their grandpa,
and their grandpa,
when he unwrapped the peeler
on Christmas morning,
told them right away
he'd known the Peeler Guy himself.

Joe. Right? Joe the Peeler Guy?
And when the kids nodded, Grandpa smiled,
wide as if it had been Santa himself
who'd slid down the chimney
and brought him that peeler in person.

IMAGINATION'S LAPSE

Ski Lodge, July, and the temps
might top a hundred.
Chair lifts motionless.
Dead silence up the slopes.

White clouds glowing at their tops,
sun's grace,
but gray ugly bellies
peel themselves up
off the peaks that drew them there.

Clouds float free
and in their drifting,
cast their shadows
over patches of hill,
measuring territory
for later.

Straw hats and bill visors
oh yes and perspiration,
shade at mid-day
coming only at a premium.

A single robin stands, hopless,
high on a rock,
looks up at the blue sky –
so blue — and seems to wonder
how much hotter it can possibly get.

Farther up the mountain,
pine trees dying in drought heat,
only the bark beetles having the last laughs,
choking needles of their prey
into brown, ignoble death.

Impossible today — even in
deepest, coldest regions
of my imaginings –
to envision snow,
conjure white-frozen panoramas
and colorful criss-crossing motion
all the way down ski trails
you can still see – etched onto the high hills.

Waiting for sunset wind to freshen,
and blow sweater-cold down the slopes,
if only for a brief moment, a shower perhaps.
A brief and cooling sleep – will freshen my mind.

INTO THE QUIET HILL NIGHT

This poem honors what was the wonderful Tucson home of
Allyn and Hugh – and the magnificent Hugh-hewn stone
sculptures that adorned its environs.

Into the quiet hill night,
and a mystical pathway opens
– out through a low and clanking gate.

Nearby and farther out, a barrel cactus,
then a tall and slender *Saguaro*, two palm trees,
a fruiting grapefruit and
wandering sprawl of grape vine
keep their silent watch over the turning earth.
All the lizards have gone to sleep.

Softly bubbling water,
down from the top of coarse granite
makes the sound of calm and freshens the air
with its cool-moistened breath.

Every once in a while along the path
a smooth stone standing silent — or soaring —
smooth stone standing out
from having shed its own rough self
into disappointed pebbles left behind,
so that only the true soul of itself remains
curved and rounded into gifted shape
emerging from under-guiding fingers
of mastering toil, polishing with final
touches of love that tested the tactile shape
of what will be left behind for the ages.

A white eagle dives earthward,
and in its plummeting frenzy
dreams the hunger dream

of tasting a death struggle
of unsuspecting tiny rat, caught unawares
in the act of seeking its own meal.

Nearby, a woman bares her softening heart
and reaches heavenward.
Her imagined alabaster arms
are suddenly capable of making the transit
to wherever it is her visions are.

Down the lane
a single slender obelisk of oiled wood
points upward — *in memoriam*,
into its own vast imaginings,
calling out its multilingual streaming prayer:
May there be peace on earth.

PURPLE AND MORE DELICATE

I turn away from the shore,
new-found stones
weighing down the sack I carry,
to make my way back up-dune to home.

A bearded drifter turns away
from his solo path along the water's edge.
He approaches, and offers up
the partial shell of a white clam,

jagged but no doubt
a seeming sort of beauty to him.
He places the shell in my open palm
and strides away, no words uttered

beyond my startled 'thank-you,'
called out to him over the surf sound.
A few minutes later,
once more he doubles back,

this time with a full-formed shell,
purple and more delicate.
Again he says nothing
and this time hurries away.

This of course is the difference.
I believe in the sea.
The drifter believes in himself,
and the encounter, and me.

PIGEONS

Honoring their duty to scatter,
they scurry on red-wire-feet;
not a single one flaps wings
or thinks to seek a higher perch.

Cotton fields of torn bread
from the wheelchaired lady;
all have resumed pecking crumbs,
as if nothing's interrupted.

One of them, self-winnowed,
follows Bedouin-style, stride-by-stride,
cocks its head to the side,
for a blinking eye contact.

Some say pigeons blink to relax;
others believe it is fear.
What color is a pigeon, anyway?
Sunlight brings out shimmers of purple,

blue-green along this one's elegant neck,
down to a nondescript body.
Nuanced royalty,
even when a parade never happens.

DARK NIGHT: PEEKSKILL

Town hill sloping up and around a slow bend,
with everybody candled indoors
and all electricity slashed off hours ago
by a single blast of thunder and
flash of blinding lightning bolt out of nowhere.

Leaving rain-drizzled silent pavement,
glistening in gun-metal slick,
all there is to show for a night
that should never have been.

The husband cut off from the wife
and trying to get to a phone
that cradles cold and black,
inside a booth that stands in front of a
clapboarded off-path delicatessen,
distinguished only by a single oversized jar
of pickled hard-boiled eggs that seemingly gleams
on a dusty shelf in a plate glass window
of a hundred years gone by.

She, trying to remember how to be patient,
he knowing all there is to know about duty,
and both wondering just how alone one can be
in a world that still contains the moon
on a clouded and starless horizon.

THE SUMMER CIRCUS COMES TO TOWN
IN DEAD OF NIGHT

The summer circus comes to town in dead of night
on silver train sliding silent onto a siding.
Nobody speaks, as clusters of townspeople
try to find their way in the dark
and keep out from under foot.
Elephants on unison command pull the tents up,
while barrel-chested men in undershirts
pound stakes that guy thick ropes into place.

Day breaks, and the breakfast tent griddles hot cakes,
fries smoky bacon and sizzling eggs, so that all can eat -
those who've created the magical camp
of the Greatest Show on Earth,
right here in the back lot of Lakeview Park
beside the Nickel Plate tracks,
and also those who tonight will play the clowns,
be shot from cannons, tame the lions,
and dazzle on trapeze and highest wire.

And the elephants, blinking their deep eyes
and swishing their gray tails,
wait to learn what it is they'll be asked to do next.

CAROUSEL

Blend of frying potatoes, vinegar,
salt from the farther sea,
taffy, turning on a silver crank across the way,
and smell of candy apple cinnamon red –

The rush and rumble and whoosh of wind, with lights
and the mirrors of lights blinking and flashing
– tattooed man in undershirt swinging from
pole to pole, snatching tickets,
eager to be done with it all.

And those horses!
Pole-bound on slippery white porcelain stalks
that disappear into black-greasy joinings
with bended cranking levers.
Always forward, and always back,
and the lift only so high
and the dip always down to predictable lows.

Looking up up into shelter of aging roof slats,
paint peeling from porchy columns,
and then, eyes closed as the diesel engine coughs
and cranks to vital speed,
and calliope takes a moment
to think about what song it will play now –
flash of light through eyelids,
horses behind closing fast!

Sometimes like the mad-mouthed painted frenzy
on glaze-bodied stallions,
flexing tails out straight for the galloping stretch –
and streaking for some semblance of victory.

Progress only in circles doubling back to beginnings

again and again and again and again.
But somehow, in the midst of it –
exhilaration – of looking back
at the open nostrils of following steeds
gaining on you.

Always one lady riding serene
on the gliding-swan bench
ankles crossed and never quite making eye contact,
dress smoothed down as if she'd been
queened some long time back
and then left to her own devices.

Off-key music steaming into every fantasy.
Rattling thump of mechanical drum and cymbal,
and reedy whistling sound of bellows calliope,
taking you back, or forward, into far far distances.

With your companion sitting side saddle
and beaming beside you
and wondering where it is that you've gone.

MARINARA CARAVAN

Truckload of onions roaring down the long hill,
skins flying up like spindrift,
followed closely by similar quantities
of ripening tomatoes.
The coveted Marinara Caravan,
heading straight for the targeted Gilroy –
Garlic Capital of the World!

In the town, everyone peers from windows,
scans the bend in the road,
anxious for the very first-ever
World Pasta Festival to begin at last.

In the town's largest parlor,
ladies in long gingham skirts
are sitting at paper-covered tea tables,
hand peeling each new clove –
chatting lightly and filling stainless bowls,
hefted by teen-aged girls.

In the shiny cauldron room, at huge benches,
the work of chopping the onions,
newly arrived, has just gotten started,
while elsewhere, gentle, knowing hands
have begun to quarter the tomatoes.

Stalks of fresh oregano and then green leaves of basil
are hauled in from wild patches up beside the lake,
by young and otherwise unruly boys,
who this day have chosen to obey their mothers.

Two burly men with perspiring forearms
crank huge grinders filled with peppercorns.
The wisest woman in town presides over the seasoning,

flicks her fingers to signal more oregano, more basil,
frowns at too much pepper, and spoons the salt herself,

from a box she carried from her own kitchen —
as huge wooden paddles, bigger than oars of lifeboats,
stir the simmering mixture down into sauce.
Next door, a young bachelor
supervises boiling fusili to perfection,
more pasta than anyone in these parts
has ever imagined.

All people everywhere stop what they're doing
and begin making their way to Gilroy.
As soon as the bread arrives,
the town will feed everyone who's hungry.

This is what they've been waiting for, to gather together,
share bounty, enjoy the rest of the day as it goes down,
perhaps to smile, even to laugh –
This is what we've all been waiting for.

SALSA FESTIVAL

But when the bus bearing the proud logo:
Eduardo Cortez y su Banda,
fresh up this morning from Mexico,
eases behind the Marinara Convoy,

I suddenly realize there might be a salsa festival
somewhere I haven't heard about.
Around the next bend perhaps an impromptu field,
with quickly constructed tables of rough wood

and vast earthen bowls, and the onions raw,
with cilantro – fine chopped by junior chefs
just now learning the art
and paying close attention to their fingers.

Cumin and Cayenne sprinkled delicate.
And sliced limes heaped strategically all about.
The tomatoes being supervised by women
wearing fancy bodices and full skirts.

And a very old woman,
having corn meal between stones,
is patting hand-fashioned tortillas
for grilling on a steel plate, over hot coals.

With joyful Eduardo and the *Banda,*
one final chorus of blaring horns
pointed directly into the sky —
everybody dancing now,
in a frenzied hunger for the freshest taste,
and all of it north of the border.

INDEPENDENCE DAY

Ribbons, tammy bunting, flapping flags
fly from porches and porticos,
festoon band shells in green parks,
taking us back to good old days

at least we think were times before
we started making so many mistakes.
Back to times it was easier
to convince us we meant well.

Dusty children with hobby horses and cap pistols
trailing red strips of spent caps,
the tiny dots burned black under silver hammers
and already scenting a universal battlefield smell.

Chasing down other dusty children,
the fleeing kids usually the younger ones
dutifully falling down *wounded* or *dead*
but only for a few seconds,

then rising in laughter or else complaining
of a premature but temporary demise,
shouting "No fair! No fair!"
Noses running at the injustice of it all.

Maybe there'd be a parade down the main street.
Streamers streaming, drums and tubas marching,
uniforms crisp and starched in the bright sun,
shoes spit-shined in the alley behind the VFW.

A picnic later, on wooden tables
covered with plastic cloths, fresh pie,
blueberry or cherry, baked beans even,
everybody laughing and eating watermelon.

It was *the rockets' red glare*
the bombs bursting in air
at the end of the day
that sealed the deal.

Sounds of celebration, same sounds now
the dreaded blasts of terror make,
as instant sparkled shrapnel
tears a tiny child from her mother's arms.

Continuing an era that should have stopped in 1945
or 1918, or maybe back to 1865, or long before.
What has gotten into us?
And why doesn't it go away?

LIFE'S POSSIBILITY

Two hundred light years away,
in the star system
they call the Bootes Constellation,

a dwarf star where life turns out to be possible
on one or more planetary globules
that spin round its dimming shimmer.

Imagine that star
out there by itself, trying hard,
with everything about to happen.

Or maybe it *has* happened
a hundred and ninety-nine light-years ago;
only the notice of it hasn't gotten to us yet,

and won't, for still another light year.
But nonetheless, those planetary globules
haven't had time yet or size

sufficient to spin themselves
into proper spheres, with equators,
and north poles, and south poles.

Continents and oceans are yet to become,
but all of this is probably on the way,
even though everything

has been so quiet there
so very very quiet
for so much of the light of those years.

Until suddenly
there's a little kid looking up and out at us,

way out there, with a smile, and maybe a laugh

that makes you want to smile back
and laugh with him
even if you *are* two hundred light years apart,

which you are, but like everything else,
such things just seem to have a way
of coming into being.

One for Each of my Grandchildren

JACK . . . AND THE WORLD WINKS BACK

*I wrote this poem when our first grandson, Jack, was
born. As he was beginning his first outbound voyage, he
was bringing me back from one of mine. It was a
stupendous time.*

JACK ! - sound of being in just the right place
and knowing full well what is going on around him,
because he is . . .

JACK - unzipped and uncurled
and popped slippery into the world,
and in such a hurry to get started, being . . .

JACK - born into a night when the full moon was hiding,
making it urgent from the very first
for him to figure out just the place
where everything's supposed to be,
including even himself, as . . .

JACK - serious and studying,
and flexing every muscle he discovers,
impatient to be on his way
and not quite being able to get there,
not quite yet, but soon, it will certainly be soon,
and then everything will be different . . .

JACK - frustrated with needing to tell you
exactly what it is he wants,
because he definitely has a plan, oh yes . . .

JACK - frustrated with needing to ask you
all the right questions all at once
needing to find all the answers just that fast . . .

JACK - pondering the world and gobbling all of it

into his careful mind,
vacuuming the whole place clean
with eyes that fix on everything and sweep it all
into this floppy catalog that grows bigger
and doubles in size inside him
every time he wakes up from a nap and lifts his head
to check things out
and see whether anything has changed yet -

JACK - with a half smile happy as a quiet pie,
snuggling his mother and
floating in love that surrounds his every move . . .

JACK - greets the troubled world,
and as it shifts its load to make room for him,
suddenly the world winks. And with a joyful gasp,
it realizes against all odds
that it has just become a better place.

TANNER

Tanner'll draw you a picture
and when you ask him what it is
he'll tell you it's a dinosaur
playing a banjo
only you can't see the banjo
'cuz it's covered with a brown sheet.
And when you tell him you can't quite
see the dinosaur, he'll tell you
that's because its under the brown sheet too!

Tanner has answers for everything,
and his favorite word as a two year old
was "actually."
Actually, he'll play you a ukulele song,
because he loves the sound the strings make.
Only you have to pretend not to listen,
or he'll stop strumming.

Tanner the good sport, plays the game,
any game, just for the playing.
Winning? Somebody wins?
That's at the end, right?
When we get to do hugs and high-fives? Okay.

Tanner, embodiment of golden retriever,
spirit of Jasmine the Dog,
mixed with all the other spirits
that make his own motor spark and sputter
and come to life in his chuckling frame.
Middle child for the time being,
solid hub of the wheel
that spins his older brother
and his little sister round him.

Tanner of the tools.
He knows how to fit things together.
He'll figure a way to build you a table,
with real screws,
or maybe a boat, or sometimes a train.

Tanner, lover of nature,
ready for ducks and geese at the pond
because he knows them all by name,
ready for turkeys at Pop-Pop's,
ready for a hippopotamus – anywhere.

Tanner of the cider press and the Easter eggs,
knew, when he was only two, to tell his Poppie
those weren't flecks of real gold
in the rocks they scrambled over in the park.
"Mica," he proclaimed, in Buster Keaton deadpan,
and shook his head at how silly
grandfathers can sometimes be.

Tanner tumbling down a snow hill, and laughing,
lying there to touch his forehead
and sometimes his tongue to the ground
just to feel what *cold* tastes like.
Or spinning his wheels in mired mud,
just to feel the whirl of water
shooting out behind his trainer-wheeled bike.

Tanner of the dress-collar shirt
and a tie of his own choosing,
dancing the train station's joy
and boats on the river,
roly-poly blond-hair, curls everywhere,
and eyes of deepest blue.

Smiling Tanner, ready for a joke,

and another joke, as long as
you'll keep laughing with him,
to cover his own darker worries.

Tanner flash-lighting his books to sleep
at the end of a play-full day
and worried just a little about the dark.
He shouldn't be worried, of course,
but he is, and sometimes he sleeps
on the floor just to be closer to the door.

Tanner, who had the chocolate fondue dream one night
and then was sad, all the day,
because he knew he'd never be lucky enough
to have the same good dream twice.

LITTLEST MADELEINE
AND THE LAKE WIND

Steady wind from the lake's horizon
creaks your screen door shut,
and as your baby, Madeleine,
dozes her afternoon sleep,
it tousles the one *perspiry* curl
that wisps on her forehead.

In her sleep she smiles,
inhales a tiny piece of the passing air
lightly into new lungs, and then
yields her breath back to the breeze.

In the doorway, you sigh, shield your eyes
from the afternoon sun,
as it begins its drowsy lapse into the lake
and then, you pull the cotton blanket up
to cover the baby's shoulder.
Everyone else tiptoes from room to room
and whispers quietly about volleyball.

The breeze, now laden
with baby's breath and sigh and whisper,
and the faintest hint of infant smell –
steals a trace of the spices from kitchen shelves
and exits, furtive, through your open window.

Up the street, that same wind when it rattles my screen,
causes my dog to bark once and then
try to take a nip from the air itself,
while I, laughing, stoop to pick up
the fluttering pages of this very poem.

The wind, now carrying infant breath and scent,

mother sigh, volley-whisper, dog bark and laughter,
– and somehow still with lake freshness on its breath –
makes its way up and over the tree line and then
down the slope and over the river bridge
to find the town, quieting into evening.

Before we begin to fix our separate suppers,
each of us, in our own time looks up
and out to the lake's horizon,
pondering the wind's beginning
and what it was that freshened its
zephyring moment and pointed it
in our direction.

As the sun finally sets,
I place a bowl of beach stones
onto the seat of the plastic patio chair
to anchor it for what might be coming.

Later, in the shadows of the deep night,
the wind, whistling under my eaves
reminds me to look out at your dark cottage
and make certain you remembered
to fasten your awnings.

ISADORA – IN FOUR VARIATIONS

1. Sonata
Isadora dances herself directly into her name.
There's always that leotard-look
that comes into her eyes
when she's pinned up her hair
and walks onto a studio floor.
For her, dancing happens in a place
well outside of worry.
"The music plays me!" she's always
happy to declare.

2. Adagio Assai
On a wintry afternoon
in a warm parlor room
with nothing to be doing,
Isadora will sit sometimes
in Lotus position, ankles crossed,
head tilted slightly back
to balance a forehead beanbag.

And then with arms extended
like wings of a swan
preparing to fly,
body forward,
neck stretched back,
she'll un-tuck one leg at a time,
then uncoil herself and slowly stand,
without disrupting the beanbag,
just to prove it can be done.

Finally, gripping the beanbag in one hand,
she will stand at the window
and watch the rain,
as it streams, slowly, down.

3. *Minuet*
Last November,
Isadora was dreaming already
of Christmas,
and snow.

She'd requested snow
on everybody's behalf,
in a letter, penned after dance class,
to Santa.

She wasn't certain
the snow would come,
but she was glad
she'd dreamed of it anyway.

4. *Rondo*
Sometimes Isadora comes down
off her pointed toes
and then becomes Izzie again.
Izzie has a foolproof way
of being sure to get a seat
on the rush-hour morning Tube
through heart-of-London
to her school in St. John's Wood,

first by acting bleary-eyed
and droopy-lid sleepy,
dragging onto the train,
reaching for a pole and then
bending her head
dramatically down to her hand.
Then, closing her eyes
she pretends to drift
almost into sleep.

Somebody always relents
to offer a seat.

As if even this
is part of the same dance
that delights her.

Two Sweat-Vision Poems

SWEAT LODGE

There would have been a first long night,
steaming rocks and sheltering tarp,
twig ribs that finally contained me
into everything, enfolding all of it,
like a quiet beast lying down to drowse,
but boiling at her belly
with all of us bustling inside.

I'd have watched you bring the rocks
and bend and tie the structure.
I would have felt the heat of the steam,
and heard its hissing.

There inside the beast, You,
all of you, and me beside you,
would have murmured into the night,
bursting in the heat of things.

In the morning, one of you
would have opened the flap
and helped me stand alone on my feet.
We would have risen in the cold dark,
and awkwardly we'd have celebrated the sun.

And the songs would have begun
to come out of my nose too,
as I stepped forward beside you
and stomped my feet into your rhythms
becoming OUR rhythms together.

Then all of you, leaving,would have left behind
rocks and tarps and dancing,
memory of perspiring shoulders touching,
late into the night, early into the morning, always.

NO SWEAT

Ancestors of my blood and of my spirit
and of all my friends who have found your balmy hill,
you who now wear the tranquil togas
and bask perspirationless
in white and breezeless wisdom,
you who murmur of deeper meanings
than I have yet to contemplate —

I need now to lie down in your arms
and feel your touch surround me
need to feel each of your fingers
graze my skin with gentle care;

I need to wonder whether any of you
sobs in the night on my behalf,
as I have done for you.

I need to feel the breath of heaven
filter through your lungs as you sigh;

I need to look up blinking against bright light
to find your clear eyes pondering me.

I need my father's father to
splash sparkling stars down upon all of us,
need my own father's soft and gentle
once-clumsy hands to reach
into my core now and cradle my heart,
smoothe its glistening surfaces, and
let me feel the healing love I once took for granted.

Ancestors of my blood and of my spirit
I need you now to chant me quiet songs in harmony,
feel your voices flow back, sounding, into my veins.

I need to find your strength and the courage
it has taken you to get to where I find you now.
Most of all I need to feel us link, fuse beyond boundaries,
so that I may go on behind mine.

ABOUT THE AUTHOR

Harry Youtt is a long-time *Plain-speech Resonance* poet. He's the author of several collections of poetry, including most recently: *Finbarr Visits the Pacific, Elderverses,* and *Outbound for Elsewhere.* In the poetry he writes, his goal is to communicate in resonant language that flows naturally. He believes the highest purpose of poetry is the clarity of communication that can enable profound absorption by as many as possible. He also believes most poetry should be looked at, again and again, the way you go back to a good photograph, to make sure you've seen and sensed everything that was there when the picture got taken.

With his wife, Judith Simon Prager, Harry has been teaching workshops in fiction and narrative non-fiction writing in the UCLA (Ext.) Writers' Program since 1990. He also occasionally conducts poetry workshops in the United States, the United Kingdom, and Ireland. His poetry is published in numerous anthologies and journals, where it has garnered a couple of national awards and several Pushcart Prize nominations. He also writes and speaks about poetry, consciousness and American culture in literary publications and at international conferences.

He has done readings of his own work in numerous locations throughout the United States and in Ireland, England, and Wales.

www.ingramcontent.com/pod-product-compliance
Lightning Source LLC
Chambersburg PA
CBHW020519030426
42337CB00011B/462